FROM THESE BEGINNINGS

Other books by the author

DON'T HOLD THEM BACK
JOHN HOSKYNS, SERJEANT-AT-LAW
THE GOSPEL

FROM THESE BEGINNINGS

*Openings of 50
Major Literary Works*

BAIRD W. WHITLOCK

SCHOCKEN BOOKS · NEW YORK

First published by Schocken Books 1985
10 9 8 7 6 5 4 3 2 1   85 86 87 88
Copyright © 1985 by Baird W. Whitlock

Library of Congress Cataloging in Publication Data
Whitlock, Baird W.
    From these beginnings.
    1. Fiction—Technique.   2. Quotations, English.
I. Title.   II. Title: Beginnings.
PN3365.W515   809.3   84–1280

Designed by Nancy Dale Muldoon
Manufactured in the United States of America
ISBN 0-8052-3908-1

PROLOGUE

ONE OF the clichés used by teachers of literature is that you can tell whether a book is going to be a good one by the time you have finished the first sentence or the first paragraph. As with most clichés, there is a good deal of substance or truth in that assertion. In the following pages we will be looking at beginnings that heralded great novels (and some near great novels). Some of the beginnings are fanciful, some philosophical, some suspenseful. All are green flags to the reader, to urge him or her on at full speed. The book is set up in such a way as to allow the reader to test his or her memory in cases of books already read, or ability to identify great writers in cases of books not yet read. For the latter, I can only hope that the openings will act as a magnet to draw the reader to those works in order to find out the wealth that is massed behind the openings. Robert Frost once said that we read good books for the one or two which will light up our lives. These are the openings of such books as have lit up men's lives through the years.

FROM THESE BEGINNINGS

C_{ALL} me Ishmael.

IN 1850, Herman Melville began work on a new book following the critical successes of *Typee, Omoo, Redburn,* and *White-Jacket.* His philosophical novel, *Mardi,* had been a terrible failure, but now he turned his attention to a whaling story that would combine a moving narrative, a scientific study of whaling, and a healthy dose of philosophy and religion. That religious tone is established in the first sentence, with the identification of the narrator, the only survivor of the quest for the great white whale, as Ishmael, the son of the unfortunate Hagar and the patriarch Abraham. Though cast aside and forced to wander in the wilderness with his mother, Ishmael was promised a rescue from his wanderings by God. The simplicity of the opening sentence belies the complexity of the novel that follows, but the reader is drawn into the story at once as he seeks to find out why Melville has named his hero after the little-known child of the sixteenth chapter of Genesis. And so begins perhaps the greatest novel in all American literature, *Moby Dick*.

*H*APPY families are all alike; every unhappy family is unhappy in its own way.

PROBABLY the most famous opening sentence in the history of the novel, this acute observation on the nature of family life opens the story of *Anna Karenina*, by Leo Tolstoy. Tolstoy began his famous 1873 novel of the emotional trials of a St. Petersburg wife who falls in love with a dashing officer soon after the public success of his even more famous novel *War and Peace*. The slightly ironic tone of the opening sentence both misleads the reader into thinking that the humorous tone of the first chapter will carry throughout the book and prepares him for the tragedy that marks Anna's attempt to escape the boredom and chill of her marriage. There is another irony to the first sentence that Tolstoy may or may not have intended. The sentence can almost as easily be reversed for an equally true statement, and it is often misquoted that way.

*O*N an evening in the latter part of May a middle-aged man was walking homeward from Shaston to the village of Marlott, in the adjoining Vale of Blakemore or Blackmoor. The pair of legs that carried him were rickety, and there was a bias in his gait which inclined him somewhat to the left of a straight line. He occasionally gave a smart nod, as if in confirmation of some opinion, though he was not thinking of anything in particular. An empty egg-basket was slung upon his arm, the nap of his hat was ruffled, a patch being quite worn away at its brim where his thumb came in taking it off. Presently he was met by an elderly parson astride on a gray mare, who, as he rode, hummed a wandering tune.

THERE is not much in this opening paragraph to tell the reader what direction the novel is to take, but the oblique walk of the man and his physical tic give an indication that nature is not quite right—or at least not quite beneficial. In 1891, Thomas Hardy published *Tess of the D'Urbervilles* as one of his series of novels on Wessex, an area of southern England that he made his own. *Tess* is subtitled "A Pure Woman," a description that many of Hardy's readers in the late Victorian period would have found challenging at the very least. They were not accustomed to think of women who had been seduced–raped and who had committed murder in quite those terms. But in a world in which the Immortals end their "sport with Tess" by seeing her hanged, matters of innocence and guilt become remarkably intertwined. It was said that "every time a novel of Thomas Hardy is published, the long arm of coincidence has to be carried in a sling for a week," and the charge of an overabundance of coincidence can easily—but not necessarily correctly—be made against the book. In the close-knit and microcosmic world of Wessex, coincidence may well be but one way of looking at reality.

T *IS* a truth universally acknowledged, that a single man in possession of a good fortune must be in want of a wife.

In 1813, a three-volume novel written "by a Lady" appeared in London. It was actually a revision of a novel written in 1797 but rejected by publishers at that time. Its author was the fine craftsman and analyst of social and family life of the age, Jane Austen. No one has examined the intricacies of family relations with more finesse or greater humor than Austen. The opening sentence states what was undoubtedly a truism among middle-class families in the early nineteenth century, but the baldness of its statement sets forth clearly the pettiness and blindness of the class of people who neither paid much attention to the Napoleonic wars raging at the time nor cared about the needs of the great majority of the people who were struggling for some kind of bearable life under the pressures of the Industrial Revolution. There is some evidence that Marx was led to many of his attitudes about class warfare by reading Austen and deciding that there was no justification for the support of such middle-class families by the labor of the working classes. The novel appearing in 1813 was entitled *Pride and Prejudice* and chronicled the attempts of the Bennet family to marry off their daughters appropriately. Elizabeth, the wittiest of the girls, becomes involved with and ultimately marries Mr. Darcy, but not until each of them can conquer the pride and prejudice that keep them apart. Luckily for both the characters and readers, love and good sense conquer all.

*W*HETHER I shall turn out to be the hero of my own life, or whether that station will be held by anybody else, these pages must show. To begin my life with the beginning of my life, I record that I was born (as I have been informed and believe) on a Friday, at twelve o'clock at night. It was remarked that the clock began to strike, and I began to cry, simultaneously.

IT IS tempting to shave the rules of this collection a bit and use the title of chapter one instead of the opening paragraph. It reads simply, "I Am Born." Indeed, many readers, when asked what the opening sentence of *David Copperfield*, by Charles Dickens, is, would reply with that title. But the first paragraph is much more revealing. This novel is more autobiographical than even Dickens was sometimes willing to admit, and his life contained both the wonderful sense of humor that he wryly reveals and the pathos that would give the newborn infant plenty of reason to cry. If the wonderful Mr. Micawber was modeled on the genuine idiosyncrasies of Dickens's father, so the tortured days of miserable child labor suffered in the warehouse of Murdstone and Grinby were an accurate description of Dickens's own childhood. Dickens has been loved and berated for over a century; loved by readers who like a good story and relish a happy ending, and berated by critics who bemoan his sentimentality, forced coincidences, and unmotivated resolutions. But no author in history has created more unforgettable characters or caused more copious tears to flow in sympathy with the downtrodden of the world. If the reader feels that happy endings are not realistic given the sordid experiences of Dickens's characters, he should remember that the author, who might well have been certified as mentally unbalanced in our own age, managed to pull himself through just such experiences to live contentedly, if not fully happily, ever after. Perhaps it was due to the fact that he recognized happiness in small but achievable goals: "Annual income twenty pounds, annual expenditure nineteen nineteen six, result happiness. Annual income twenty pounds, annual expenditure twenty pounds ought and six, result misery."

*M*OTHER died today. Or, maybe, yesterday; I can't be sure. The telegram from the Home says: YOUR MOTHER PASSED AWAY. FUNERAL TOMORROW. DEEP SYMPATHY. Which leaves the matter doubtful; it could have been yesterday.

THE STRANGER was Albert Camus's first novel, written at the age of twenty-nine, in 1942, after an active career in journalism, the theater, and the French Resistance. In the latter, he edited an important underground paper, *Combat*. The indecisiveness expressed in the opening paragraph is an appropriate beginning for the life of the hero of the tale, Mersault, a Frenchman in Algiers. For many readers Mersault is the perfect fictional example of existentialism, and wherever that philosophical school is studied in literature courses, this novel is a required part of the syllabus. Camus claimed that he was misjudged and that he did not consider himself an existentialist. But Mersault's attitudes and behavior constantly reflect an unwillingness to substitute his own experience—or any other individual's experience—for universal truth. Mersault's only real anger is triggered by another person's (the priest's) attempt to define a universal truth. But Mersault does not deny the reality of his own experience. In that experience lies the only genuine existence he can describe. So whether or not Camus wished to see his work as a statement of existentialism, that is what it turns out to be.

I *FIRST* met him in Piraeus. I wanted to take the boat for Crete and had gone down to the port. It was almost daybreak and raining. A strong *sirocco* was blowing the spray from the waves as far as the little café, whose glass doors were shut. The café reeked of brewing sage and human beings whose breath steamed the windows because of the cold outside. Five or six seamen, who had spent the night there, muffled in their brown goatskin reefer-jackets, were drinking coffee or sage and gazing out of the misty windows at the sea. The fish, dazed by the blows of the raging waters, had taken refuge in the depths, where they were waiting till calm was restored above. The fishermen crowding in the cafés were also waiting for the end of the storm, when the fish, reassured, would rise to the surface after the bait. Soles, hog fish and skate were returning from their nocturnal expeditions. Day was now breaking.

A FAR greater number of people have seen that opening than have read it, for the movie version of *Zorba the Greek* has been far more popular than the novel by Nikos Kazantzakis. The opening in that storm-tossed café was caught on film exactly as the author intended. If the cameras did not then descend into the Saronic Gulf to catch the migrating fish, it was due to the fact that the film had other, just as successful, ways of showing the link of the fisherman Zorba to animal life and animal vitality. *Zorba* appeared in an English translation in 1952, five years before Kazantzakis's death, but the author was not able to see the famous film based on his work, for it was not made until 1964. It is relatively easy to get an argument started on the relative merits of the book and film, but almost no one disagrees about the power of the work or the power of the principal character. His vitality is overwhelming. Those who have only seen the film are missing a good deal, and those who have never read any of Kazantzakis are missing one of the most versatile writers of this century.

*I*N A village of La Mancha, which I prefer to leave unnamed, there lived not long ago one of those gentlemen that keep a lance in the lance-rack, an old shield, a lean hack, and a greyhound for hunting. A stew of rather more beef than mutton, hash on most nights, bacon and eggs on Saturdays, lentils on Fridays, and a pigeon or so extra on Sundays consumed three quarters of his income. The rest went for a coat of fine cloth and velvet breeches and shoes to match for holidays, while on weekdays he cut a fine figure in his best homespun. He had in his house a housekeeper past forty, a niece under twenty, and a lad for the field and marketplace, who saddled the hack as well as handled the pruning knife. The age of this gentleman of ours was bordering on fifty. He was of a hardy constitution, spare, gaunt-featured, a very early riser, and fond of hunting. . . .

I HAVE cheated a bit by leaving the first paragraph unfinished. The reason, of course, is that Miguel de Cervantes then goes into a discussion of the name of the hero, Don Quixote. Whether *Don Quixote* is called a novel, a mock epic, a romance, or whatever, is a matter for literary critics to argue about. For the general reader it is a sheer delight. The Don, lean as the unfortunate steed (Rosinante) that he rides, and his faithful sidekick Sancho Panza have ridden into history as two of those rare literary creations, genuine originals like Hamlet and Falstaff. The comparison with Shakespeare is not an idle one. Although Cervantes was born seventeen years before his English contemporary, they both died in the same year, 1616. At about the same time as Shakespeare was staging *Hamlet,* Cervantes was probably beginning the story of the Don while in prison, where he unfortunately had to do much of his writing because of his frequent struggles with the authorities. The first part of the Don's history was published in 1605 and the second part in 1615. The opening of the book certainly creates an interest in the mild-mannered, impoverished nobleman with his interest in medieval romances, but it does not prepare us for the lasting message of this great book: in an insane world, only those who appear insane can be truly wise.

WHAN that April with his showres soote
The droughte of March hath perced to the roote,
And bathed every veine in swich licour,
Of which vertu engendred is the flowr;
Whan Zephyrus eek with his sweete breeth
Inspired hath in every holt and heeth
The tendre croppes, and the yonge sonne
Hath in the Ram his halve cours yronne,
And smale fowles maken melodye
That sleepen al the night with open ye—
So priketh hem Nature in hir corages—
Thanne longen folk to goon on pilgrimages,
And palmeres for to seeken straunge strondes
To ferne halwes, couthe in sondry londes;
And specially from every shires ende
Of Engelond to Canterbury they wende,
The holy blisful martyr for to seeke
That hem hath holpen whan that they were seke.

MEMORIZED by generations of high-school and college students in an effort by teachers to get the young to "hear" Middle English before they try to read it, these first eighteen lines of Geoffrey Chaucer's *The Canterbury Tales* introduce us to the landscape, animal life, and religious customs of medieval England. By the time we have finished this single-sentence opening paragraph, we are ready for the zest for life as well as the religious positions of the motley group of pilgrims that gather at the Tabard, perhaps in 1386, when Chaucer apparently first came up with the idea for his wonderful set of stories. But accurate though the picture of these medieval wanderers may be, it is their more eternal characteristics that win us to them. As Dryden was to observe three centuries later, "Here is God's plenty." We may wonder at the motivation of some of these pilgrims, be alienated by some of their methods (especially those of some of the "religious" figures), even be bored by some of the long tales they tell, but we, like Chaucer, love to be in their company. Moreover, we recognize that Chaucer has given us a group of people with whom we can still identify today, and we learn to understand and even to bear with some of our own contemporaries better because Chaucer has taught us how to understand and bear with his fellow travelers.

*I*N MY younger and more vulnerable years my father gave me some advice that I've been turning over in my mind ever since.

"Whenever you feel like criticizing any one," he told me, "just remember that all the people in this world haven't had the advantages that you've had."

THE narrator of the novel *The Great Gatsby*, by F. Scott Fitzgerald, follows his father's advice. As he says in the following paragraph, "In consequence, I'm inclined to reserve all judgments, a habit that has opened up many curious natures to me and also made me the victim of not a few veteran bores." Jay Gatsby, the hero of the book, may be one of the many curious natures, but he is certainly not one of the veteran bores. The novel, published midway through the twenties, is in many ways as good as or even better a depiction of the lost generation than Hemingway's *The Sun Also Rises*. Gatsby represents some of the best as well as many of the worst qualities of his age. Meanwhile, Nick Carraway watches from his spectator distance the social convolutions of Daisy, Jay, Tom, and the rest of Long Island society, as it drives itself (both figuratively and literally) to death. Taken pretty generally as a good description of East Coast society during the Roaring Twenties when it first appeared, *The Great Gatsby* has grown in critical stature through the years, and it is now considered to be one of America's greatest novels. Whether it will remain in that high position is a question that only time and more generations of readers will tell.

*M*Y father had a small estate in Nottinghamshire; I was the third of five sons. He sent me to Emanuel College in Cambridge, at fourteen years old, where I resided three years, and applied my self close to my studies: but the charge of maintaining me (although I had a very scanty allowance) being too great for a narrow fortune, I was bound apprentice to Mr. James Bates, an eminent surgeon in London, with whom I continued four years; and my father now and then sending me small sums of money, I laid them out in learning navigation, and other parts of the mathematics, useful to those who intend to travel, as I always believed it would be some time or other my fortune to do. When I left Mr. Bates, I went down to my father; where, by the assistance of him and my uncle John, and some other relations, I got forty pounds, and a promise of thirty pounds a year to maintain me at Leyden: there I studied physic two years and seven months, knowing it would be useful in long voyages.

WITH such a matter-of-fact beginning, the reader sets forth on one of the, if not *the* greatest of all travel stories in the English language in the company of Lemuel Gulliver. He also sets forth in the company of the father of modern English prose style, Jonathan Swift, the Church of England priest and author of *Gulliver's Travels,* or, more accurately, *Travels into several Remote Nations of the World.* The tone of stodgy accuracy and detail of the opening provides the same wonderful contrast to the imaginary and imaginative world of places like Lilliput as the apparent clarity of Swift's geographical location of his ports of visit: Lilliput, for example, is exactly at the latitude of "30 degrees 2 minutes south." Of course, we are given no longitude to plot the spot. Too many readers feel that they have read *Gulliver's Travels* because they were introduced to it in school or in the movies; they have not. They have met up only with an antiseptic or sterilized version. They have not met Gulliver trying to find the answer to the lack of toilet facilities in his prison, or the mirth of the marching soldiers of Lilliput as they look up in admiration at Gulliver's torn pants crotch as they march between the triumphal arch of his spread legs. And they have usually not understood the bitterness and perception of Swift's political satire. They probably haven't even witnessed Gulliver's amazing fire-fighting abilities when he tries to save the Queen's apartments. Perhaps more important, most readers never get beyond Lilliput and miss the grotesqueries of Brobdingnag, the science-gone-haywire of Laputa, and the real misanthropism of the voyage to the Houyhnhnms. None of the imagination and fantasy would be half so effective were it not for the phlegmatic ordinariness of the hero who reveals himself in the opening paragraph.

*I*N THE middle of the journey of our life I came to myself in a dark wood where the straight way was lost.

PERHAPS it is unfair to use a prose translation for the opening of one of the greatest poems in any language, but the Carlyle-Wicksteed translation catches the majesty of the opening tercet of Dante's monumental *Divine Comedy* from the early fourteenth century. Dante begins his imagined journey into Hell at the age of thirty-five, on Good Friday, 1300, and with the start of that journey, as one critic has remarked, the modern world begins. But as the reader soon discovers, the person lost in midlife is not only a Florentine named Dante Alighieri, but every man; the time is not only the Middle Ages, but any age. It can only be hoped that the reader comes through to the same understanding of his situation in life and the same enlightenment as Dante did. Unfortunately, this is one of those great works that really needs to be read with copious footnotes in order to be understood at any real depth. But Dante is so powerful, his images so concrete and realistic, that he sweeps the reader along with him in spite of the multitude of historical references. We cannot, or should not, be the same as we once were after we have finished the book. Dante immediately became recognized as one of the greatest poets in history, and his book became a source of information, of study and meditation, and of inspiration. For the modern reader who has been led to believe that educated people before Columbus thought the world was flat, it is important to remember that no reader of Dante—and that included almost anyone who could read at all—could believe that nonsense. Dante and his readers knew that the world was a sphere, and Columbus had only one danger in sailing to China: not of falling off the edge, but of bumping into the Mount of Purgatory on the way.

1801.-I HAVE just returned from a visit to my landlord—the solitary neighbour that I shall be troubled with. This is certainly a beautiful country! In all England, I do not believe that I could have fixed on a situation so completely removed from the stir of society. A perfect misanthropist's Heaven—and Mr Heathcliff and I are such a suitable pair to divide the desolation between us. A capital fellow! He little imagined how my heart warmed towards him when I beheld his black eyes withdraw so suspiciously under their brows, as I rode up, and when his fingers sheltered themselves, with a jealous resolution still further in his waistcoat, as I announced my name.

PERHAPS it is too strong to say that the reader is aware by the end of the first paragraph of the relative emptiness of this town-bred speaker in comparison with the passion and inner fire of the master of Wuthering Heights, but certainly by the end of the first page, he knows which one to pay attention to. Gradually Emily Brontë draws us into the story, first from the point of view of the outsider, then from the point of view of the local housekeeper, Mrs. Dean, and then into the passionate relationship of Heathcliff and Cathy which forms the heart of the novel *Wuthering Heights,* published in 1847, a year before Emily's death. The novel appeared as the work of Ellis Bell, just as Charlotte Brontë's work appeared under the name of Currer Bell. These daughters of the parish priest of Haworth felt it important to mask their identities as women in order for their works to be taken seriously. Perhaps Emily felt an even greater need to shelter her pagan passion under a pseudonym. Brought up in the rectory of the church in the village that careens downhill in narrow streets cramped on both sides by the grey stone, adjoined houses of the villagers, Emily could brush through the windbreak of the rectory garden and find herself in the wild desolation of the Yorkshire moors. It is that desolation and the turbulent emotions that it could stir in the hearts and souls of outwardly dour folk that she described so well in the novel. The outside world, in the figure of the opening speaker, Mr. Lockwood, could not understand that inner power and torment, but the reader eventually can as Emily Brontë takes us inside the souls of her characters and forces us to feel with them, even though we may never feel like them.

*T*HERE was in Westphalia, in the castle of the Baron Thunder-ten-tronckh, a young man to whom nature had given the most pleasant manners. His features declared his soul. He had quite good judgment, with the most simple mind; it is, I think, for this reason that he was named Candide. The older servants of the house suspected that he was the son of the baron's sister and a good and honest gentleman of the region, whom that lady never wished to marry because he could prove only seventy-one quarterings, and the rest of his genealogical tree had been lost through the ravages of .
time.

FRANÇOIS Marie Arouet—Voltaire—published *Candide* first in 1759, but he did not sign his name to it or admit that it was his work. By 1761, when he made some extensive additions, the book had already reached the fame that it has held ever since as one of the most effective satires of all time. The simple-minded Candide is a perfect foil for the many philosophies of life foisted upon him by his associates, especially his tutor Pangloss's repetition of Leibniz's statement that "Everything is for the best in the best of worlds." Even in his first paragraph, Voltaire manages to set the stage for the incongruity of human behavior which, for all the wrong reasons, keeps itself from happiness. But if the baron's sister refused a happy marriage because of silly social snobbery, she is hardly in the same class as the pillagers, rapists, murderers, and other light-hearted humans who fill the pages of this short book. Only in Eldorado, located high in the mountains of Peru, are there people who have their values straight and treat one another decently. It is interesting to the modern reader who tends to regard the roots of our culture as being in European civilization to find that Voltaire, in his description of Eldorado, was simply using the letters and books of missionaries and travelers among the Indian tribes as a source of his description. Perhaps we have been looking in the wrong place for our models of behavior. But Voltaire is wise enough to conclude that if we are to find peace in our own civilization, we must learn to "cultivate our own garden."

$O_{N\ AN}$ exceptionally hot evening early in July a young man came out of the garret in which he lodged in S. Place and walked slowly, as though in hesitation, towards K. bridge.

He had successfully avoided meeting his landlady on the staircase. His garret was under the roof of a high, five-storied house and was more like a cupboard than a room. The landlady who provided him with garret, dinners, and attendance, lived on the floor below, and every time he went out he was obliged to pass her kitchen, the door of which invariably stood open. And each time he passed, the young man had a sick, frightened feeling, which made him scowl and feel ashamed. He was hopelessly in debt to his landlady, and was afraid of meeting her.

This was not because he was cowardly and abject, quite the contrary; but for some time past he had been in an overstrained irritable condition, verging on hypochondria. He had become so completely absorbed in himself, and isolated from his fellows that he dreaded meeting, not only his landlady, but any one at all. He was crushed by poverty, but the anxieties of his position had of late ceased to weigh upon him. He had given up attending to matters of practical importance; he had lost all desire to do so. Nothing that any landlady could do had a real terror for him. But to be stopped on the stairs, to be forced to listen to her trivial, irrelevant gossip, to pestering demands for payment, threats and complaints, and to rack his brains for excuses, to prevaricate, to lie—no, rather than that, he would creep down the stairs like a cat and slip out unseen.

THE usual way critics differentiate between Tolstoy and his compatriot Fyodor Dostoyevsky is to call Tolstoy a horizontal narrator and Dostoyevsky a vertical narrator. Whether or not that comparison is fair to Tolstoy is not the issue here; the description of Dostoyevsky is an accurate one. It is for that reason that I have used the first three paragraphs of his masterpiece *Crime and Punishment*. Nowhere is there a better example of the method Dostoyevsky uses than this opening. The reader begins with an unexceptional surface action, lunges downward into the surroundings that work on his mind, and then plunges into the confused and turbulent psyche of the student Raskolnikov, where he will largely remain for the rest of the book. Dostoyevsky worked at a feverish pace during the years 1864 to 1866 in order to finish this book as a way of getting out of debt. When the book appeared in 1866, it was an immediate success and has been recognized ever since as one of the great classics of world literature. There are some readers who are not satisfied by the rather conservative religious resolution of the novel, but the quiet acceptance of God through the experience of suffering imprisonment in Siberia had a very realistic model in the life of the author himself. For those who sometimes question the violence of the internal passions that Dostoyevsky presents to us, it is helpful to remember that Sigmund Freud said that in the presence of a writer like Dostoyevsky, all a psychologist or psychoanalyst could do is bow down in admiration for such insight.

*M*Y true name is so well known in the records or registers at Newgate, and in the Old Bailey, and there are some things of such consequence still depending there, relating to my particular conduct, that it is not to be expected I should set my name or the account of my family to this work; perhaps, after my death, it may be better known; at present it would not be proper, no, not though a general pardon should be issued, even without exceptions and reserve of persons or crimes.

ONE of the never-ending battles among literary scholars is the question of which book was the first novel in the English language. Probably *Moll Flanders*, by Daniel Defoe, can stake the earliest claim to that title. Written by Defoe in 1722, the book set out to describe in the most realistic terms possible the life of a young woman of easy virtue who was an early model for the popular phrase "More sinned against than sinning." Defoe's subtitle says it all: "Who was Born in Newgate, and during a Life of continu'd Variety for Threescore Years, besides her Childhood, was Twelve Year a Whore, five times a Wife (whereof once to her own Brother), Twelve Year a Thief, Eight Year a Transported Felon in Virginia, at last grew Rich, liv'd Honest, and died a Penitent, Written from her own Memorandums . . ." Defoe's productivity at this point in his life was amazing: four other works appeared in the same year, one of which was the powerful *A Journal of the Plague Year*, a work which places Defoe solidly in the development of modern journalism. The same sense of reality and documentary exposition which characterizes the *Journal* is apparent in the opening of *Moll*. The modern reader ought to feel at home with the legal restraint of Moll's self-introduction after reading any of the Watergate group's revelations from their cells. But I would hope that they would equally feel themselves in the presence of a much finer writer.

*A*S I walked through the wilderness of this world, I lighted on a certain place where was a Den, and I laid me down in that place to sleep: and as I slept I dreamed a dream. I dreamed, and behold I saw a man clothed with rags, standing in a certain place, with his face from his own house, a book in his hand, and a great burden upon his back. I looked, and saw him open the book and read therein; and as he read, he wept and trembled; and not being able longer to contain, he brake out with a lamentable cry, saying, "What shall I do?"

As I was growing up, I was told by my teachers that the two most-printed books in the world were the Bible and John Bunyan's *The Pilgrim's Progress*. I have no reason to doubt the truth of that remark, although I tend to believe that Bunyan no longer comes close to maintaining his former high position. The book was started while Bunyan was serving a jail term in 1675 for preaching without a license, but it was not published until 1678. In its recounting of the conversion of its hero, Christian, and his subsequent travails in reaching the Celestial City, the book succeeds in setting forth one of the clearest and most moving allegories ever written. It is, as has been proven over the years, a textbook example of that literary form. But it is far more than that. For any Christian it is a spiritual autobiography. The allegorical experiences are real experiences, not fictional creations. But the book is also more than that or it would not have retained its power in an age of doubt. It is a rollicking good story with good and evil characters, genuine dangers, real terrors, and all the obvious seductions of the Vanity Fair of the world.

I WISH either my father or my mother, or indeed both of them, as they were in duty both equally bound to it, had minded what they were about when they begot me; had they duly consider'd how much depended upon what they were then doing;—that not only the production of a rational Being was concern'd in it, but that possibly the happy formation and temperature of his body, perhaps his genius and the very cast of his mind;—and, for aught they knew to the contrary, even the fortunes of his whole house might take their turn from the humours and dispositions which were then uppermost:—Had they duly weighed and considered all this, and proceeded accordingly,—I am verily persuaded I should have made a quite different figure in the world, from that, in which the reader is likely to see me.—Believe me, good folks, this is not so inconsiderable a thing as many of you may think it;—you have all, I dare say, heard of the animal spirits, as how they are transfused from father to son, &c. &c.—and a great deal to that purpose:—Well, you may take my word, that nine parts in ten of a man's sense or his nonsense, his successes and miscarriages in this world depend upon their motions and activity, and the different tracks and trains you put them into; so that when they are once set a-going, whether right or wrong, 'tis not a halfpenny matter,—away they go cluttering like hey-go-mad; and by treading the same steps over and over again, they presently make a road of it, as plain and as smooth as a garden-walk, which, when they are once used to, the Devil himself sometimes shall not be able to drive them off it.

Pray, my dear, quoth my mother, *have you not forgot to wind up the clock?*—*Good G—!* cried my father, making an exclamation, but taking care to moderate his voice at the same time,—*Did ever woman, since the creation of the world, interrupt a man with such a silly question?* Pray, what was your father saying?—Nothing.

37

IF anyone is in the slightest doubt about the truth of Solomon's dictum that there is nothing new under the sun, a reading of Laurence Sterne's *Tristram Shandy* should set him straight. Hitting the reading public in 1760, this madcap novel by a Yorkshire clergyman followed the first absolutely clear and obvious novel, Samuel Richardson's *Pamela*, by a mere twenty years, but it is as modern in form and approach as the most avant-garde novel of the twentieth century. As the perceptive reader soon discovers, the story line moves from conception (strangely interrupted as that may be) to circumcision, but in that sometimes concealed chronology, it wanders back through history and forward to later events in the hero's life. Nowhere has the reader been taken more openly into the framework of a story. Sterne talks to him (or her, as his main object of attention is a lady reader) constantly, making suggestions of passages to be skipped (only, it must be added, to the great loss of the reader), offering visual aids to understanding (?), commenting on passages to be read with care or repeated, and generally making the reader a part of the narrative itself. Perhaps the novel is for older readers. I can remember being bored with it when I was in college; now I can only be amazed at my own obtuseness. But whatever the age of the reader, he must give himself up to the author, surrender to the flow of the book, and just relax, enjoying the play, delighting in characters like Uncle Toby. It is an experience of pure joy—and sometimes almost as shocking as it must have been to the eighteenth-century readers who created the need for five editions in the twenty years following its first publication.

*I*T WAS late in the evening when K. arrived. The village was deep in snow. The Castle hill was hidden, veiled in mist and darkness, nor was there even a glimmer of light to show that a castle was there. On the wooden bridge leading from the main road to the village, K. stood for a long time gazing into the illusory emptiness above him.

PROBABLY with no other writer is the reader left so mystified, at least at the beginning of a story, as with Franz Kafka. We stand with K. as we stood alone ourselves on our entrance to the world. If we are not sure that heaven, or a Castle, exists because we can't at first see it nor, in spite of all our efforts, reach it, we are equally unsure whether the world we have reached, or the village, is real or illusory. All options are open as Kafka begins his tale of the land surveyor who has come, or been called—the reader is never sure which—to the village in order to take up his job. What *The Castle* means is argued about by every reader who approaches the book. For some it is a book about religion, for others about psychology, for others about government. Probably all are right. (No one who has tried to make his way around Prague for any length of time would question Kafka's description of bureaucracy.) Kafka wrote this book in 1918, but like his other two novels, *The Trial* and *Amerika*, it was not published during his lifetime. He never completed the ending. Six years later, at the age of forty-one, this incredibly gifted thinker and stylist was buried in his native city of Prague.

*O*URS is essentially a tragic age, so we refuse to take it tragically. The cataclysm has happened, we are among the ruins, we start to build up new little habits, to have new little hopes. It is rather hard work: there is now no smooth road into the future: but we go round, or scramble over the obstacles. We've got to live, no matter how many skies have fallen.

IF YOU guessed this one right, go celebrate and treat yourself to a special drink or meal. It would be hard to guess on the basis of this great beginning about the state of the world following the First World War that when I first wanted to read this book, I had to get special permission from the Head Librarian at Rutgers University, and then had to sit in the locked cage on the top floor of the library to read it, as the book was not allowed in general circulation. The world has changed as far as acceptance of the book is concerned, although it would be hard to challenge the continuing validity of the opening paragraph. In 1928, in Florence, Italy, the British writer D. H. Lawrence published his famous—or infamous, depending on your position—*Lady Chatterley's Lover*. This first paragraph should challenge any reader who thinks the work was intentionally pornographic to think again. For either Lawrence was out to fool the world by inserting such a serious opening or his book is about a good deal more than the overtly stated sexual encounters between Lady Chatterley and her husband's gamekeeper, Mellors. The truth is obviously the second. The fact that so few people will be able to identify the opening is probably an indication that even among serious readers, there is still the tendency to approach this book for its sensational reputation rather than for its inherent literary worth. However, Lawrence's *Lady Chatterley* is safe wherever the presence of socially redeeming content is the test of whether or not a work is to be regarded as pornographic.

"*THE* Bottoms" succeeded to "Hell Row". Hell Row was a block of thatched, bulging cottages that stood by the brookside on Greenhill Lane. There lived the colliers who worked in the little gin-pits two fields away. The brook ran under the alder-trees, scarcely soiled by these small mines, whose coal was drawn to the surface by donkeys that plodded wearily in a circle round a gin. And all over the countryside were these same pits, some of which had been worked in the time of Charles II, the few colliers and donkeys burrowing down like ants into the earth, making queer mounds and little black places among the corn-fields and the meadows. And the cottages of these coalminers, in blocks and pairs here and there, together with odd farms and homes of the stockingers, straying over the parish, formed the village of Bestwood.

PROBABLY the only thing that would mislead the reader in identifying this paragraph is its position in this book, directly following a work by D. H. Lawrence. The reader may think, "Well, it sounds like Lawrence, but he wouldn't put two by the same author right next to each other." Well, "he" did. And this 1913 opening to *Sons and Lovers* is far more typical of Lawrence than the beginning of *Lady Chatterley*. We are introduced immediately into the world in which Lawrence grew up, for *Sons and Lovers* is his most autobiographical novel. If we are not yet aware of the oedipal relations of the hero with his father and mother, we are certainly already sure of the crushing influence of the coalmining district on its inhabitants, both human and animal. And yet there is still hope that nature will survive, just as the cornfields and meadows manage to survive around the hellholes of the colliery pits.

*H*OW do people get to this clandestine Archipelago? Hour by hour planes fly there, ships steer their course there, and trains thunder off to it—but all with nary a mark on them to tell of their destination. And at ticket windows or at travel bureaus for Soviet or foreign tourists the employees would be astounded if you were to ask for a ticket to go there. They know nothing and they've never heard of the Archipelago as a whole or of any one of its innumerable islands.

THE unsuspecting reader of this paragraph might well think he or she is about to embark on a piece of Russian science fiction, but unfortunately for all of us, that is not the case. Instead, the reader is being introduced to a very real world, the world of Russian detention camps and political prisoners. For anyone who has read Aleksandr Solzhenitsyn's *One Day in the Life of Ivan Denisovich* first, the two long volumes of his *The Gulag Archipelago*, from which this opening paragraph is taken, reveal that there is little "fictional" about his short novel, except perhaps that there is some lightness in the novel that is not present in the real world of the prisons; but there is courage, and conviction, and even heroism. I was once asked by a Czech friend who had refused to sign the Petition of 1977 whether I was not ashamed of her. I asked her whether she had read the *Gulag*, and she said she had, although she did not explain how she had managed that while living in Prague. I then referred her to the passage in which Solzhenitsyn pointed out that no one who had undergone the pressures and nightmares of the camps and prisons could ever *blame* anyone for collapsing under those pressures. It is a world in which Kafka's literary nightmares are far more real than the sanitized world that most of us encounter. The *Gulag* is not an easy book, either in length or in message, but it is a necessity for anyone who wants to face the realities of our age with honesty. The work was started in 1956 and published in the United States in 1973. It is, unfortunately, still very much up to date.

*W*HAT made me take this trip to Africa? There is no quick explanation. Things got worse and worse and worse and pretty soon they were too complicated.

When I think of my condition at the age of fifty-five when I bought the ticket, all is grief. The facts begin to crowd me and soon I get a pressure in the chest. A disorderly rush begins—my parents, my wives, my girls, my children, my farm, my animals, my habits, my money, my music lessons, my drunkenness, my prejudices, my brutality, my teeth, my face, my soul! I have to cry, "No, no, get back, curse you, let me alone!" But how can they let me alone? They belong to me. They are mine. And they pile into me from all sides. It turns into chaos.

47

PROBABLY the first paragraph would be enough to make the point of the opening of Saul Bellow's marvelous novel *Henderson the Rain King*, which appeared in various segments in 1958 but was not published as a whole until the following year. If there is any reader who cannot identify with at least half of the list of pressures that Bellow enumerates, he may not appreciate the wild abandon of the book, but he also may not be fully human. Henderson may be larger than life, but he also lives to the full, and he drags the reader with him through the turbulence. The date of publication is interesting, for the book takes the reader from the world of the Second World War, which Bellow had chronicled in *Augie March*, through the moral ambiguities of the 1950s, and introduces or prepares for the chaos of the 1960s. Bellow has many fine novels to his credit, but none more full of life, zest, and humor than *Henderson*.

A SQUAT grey building of only thirty-four stories. Over the main entrance the words, CENTRAL LONDON HATCHERY AND CONDITIONING CENTRE, and, in a shield, the World State's motto, COMMUNITY, IDENTITY, STABILITY.

The enormous room on the ground floor faced towards the north. Cold for all the summer beyond the panes, for all the tropical heat of the room itself, a harsh thin light glared through the windows, hungrily seeking some draped lay figure, some pallid shape of academic goose-flesh, but finding only the glass and nickel and bleakly shining porcelain of a laboratory. Wintriness responded to wintriness. The overalls of the workers were white, their hands gloved with a pale corpse-coloured rubber. The light was frozen, dead, a ghost. Only from the yellow barrels of the microscopes did it borrow a certain rich and living substance, lying along the polished tubes like butter, streak after luscious streak in long recession down the work tables.

THE influence of Aldous Huxley's *Brave New World* has been so widespread, the accuracy of his 1932 prophecy so exact, that the original impact of his opening has been somewhat lost to the modern reader. So many science fiction novels have tried to recreate the soulless mechanical world that Huxley sets forth in his opening that the first paragraph could be the start of hundreds of other books. But the true artist comes through in the second paragraph. The irony of the death images in the place of birth in the new society is set forth in unforgettable terms. Few writers would have thought of the visual connection with butter and the description of that color as luscious in the stainless steel environment of the Fertilizing Room of the new society. I spent an afternoon with Huxley shortly before his death, and we spoke of the fact that he had been surprised about only one thing connected with the prophetic elements contained in this book: they had all come true far sooner than he had foreseen. And there is almost nothing in the way of Huxley's prophetic medication, attitudes toward birth and death, substitute religions, or decay of humane culture that has not come to pass since the early 1930s. Many readers were horrified when Orwell's *1984* appeared with its grim prophecy of the world of Newspeak (which has become the official language of most national governments these days), but *Brave New World* remains, for me, the most frightening of all science fiction projections, for most people really want it to happen. And happen it has, from test-tube babies, to green Malthusian belts, to television-centered death wards, to trip-inducing drugs, to socially accepted group therapy orgies, to the ever-present tranquilizer.

*A*N unassuming young man was travelling, in midsummer, from his native city of Hamburg to Davos-Platz in the Canton of the Grisons, on a three weeks' visit.

THIS opening sentence-paragraph is a kind of test case for the thesis of this book. There is certainly nothing mysterious, ecstatic, or even humorous in this plain beginning of what looks like a plain journey for a very plain gentleman. It would have been intellectually spicier to quote from the Foreword one of my favorite sentences on memory and intellectual history: "Is not the pastness of the past the more complete, the more profound, the more legendary, the nearer before the present that it falls?" That is the sort of problem that Thomas Mann's 1924 novel, *The Magic Mountain*, sets before the reader on page after page. One philosophy professor of mine described the book as "the gauntlet of the human spirit," and I have never heard a better description. The young man from Hamburg must run the gauntlet of all the basic questions human beings have asked each other through the ages as he encounters the intellectual combatants Naphta and Settembrini, the representatives of northern Europe and the Mediterranean, the Gothic and the Renaissance, the Classicist and the Romantic. Actually, the opening sentence is remarkably apt for the kind of narrative that we are given. The plot has been summarized as: "A young man goes to visit his cousin at a TB sanatorium in Switzerland for three weeks and spends seven years." That's not a bad synopsis. Another critic has said of Mann as a storyteller that he is the kind of man who invites you for a walk and about every ten feet suggests sitting down for a few minutes and discussing an idea, which takes half an hour. He stretches your mind and your imagination. He deals in history and philosophy, but he also touches on the occult and the psychoanalytic. All learning is, indeed, his province, and just as the rather dull Hans Castorp is wrenched from his dullness and provincialism, so the reader is lifted into a genuine educational search and quest that will alter his perceptions and sensitivity ever after.

*I*N THE late summer of that year we lived in a house in a village that looked across the river and the plain to the mountains. In the bed of the river there were pebbles and boulders, dry and white in the sun, and the water was clear and swiftly moving and blue in the channels. Troops went by the house and down the road and the dust they raised powdered the leaves of the trees. The trunks of the trees too were dusty and the leaves fell early that year and we saw the troops marching along the road and the dust rising and leaves, stirred by the breeze, falling and the soldiers marching and afterward the road bare and white except for the leaves.

PROBABLY the most quoted beginning paragraph in twentieth-century American prose, this passage from Ernest Hemingway's 1929 war narrative *A Farewell to Arms* has been reprinted in nearly every freshman rhetoric book since the 1930s. It is quintessential Hemingway: bare, stark, and muscular. Everything is verbs and nouns. Where adjectives do occur, they are placed in predicate positions so that they gain the appearance of nouns or substantives. Commas are omitted in order to give the sense of simultaneity over stretches of time. In some ways Hemingway's description feels like a Monet landscape or painting of a seacoast town. The pure colors are dabbed on the canvas, and the eye of the beholder mixes them; so too with Hemingway's picture. Unfortunately, his style became too standard and began to mimic itself. And probably no modern author has been more copied and parodied. But in this novel, as in the preceding novel of the lost generation, *The Sun Also Rises*, the style works. The tautness even extends to the title itself, for the farewell is to both military arms and the arms of the dead Catherine Barkley, just as the novel itself is half a war story and half a romance. If the opening paragraph can claim remarkable fame, it must share that fame with the equally well-known final sentence, "After a while I went out and left the hospital and walked back to the hotel in the rain."

*T*HROUGH the fence, between the curling flower spaces, I could see them hitting. They were coming toward where the flag was and I went along the fence. Luster was hunting in the grass by the flower tree. They took the flag out, and they were hitting. Then they put the flag back and they went to the table, and he hit and the other hit. Then they went on, and I went along the fence. Luster came away from the flower tree and we went along the fence and they stopped and we stopped and I looked through the fence while Luster was hunting in the grass.

THE last sentence of this opening paragraph begins to approach the form that Clifton Fadiman once described as "Faulkner's non-stop or 'life' sentence." I often wonder if there is any other reader as dumb or nonobservant as I was the first time I read William Faulkner's *The Sound and the Fury*. I was nearly through the novel, which is told from the varying points of view of the major characters, before I came to the realization of why the simple-minded Benjy, who loved the pasture, his sister Caddy, and firelight, spent his time wandering along the fence at the edge of the golf course. I just never paid attention to the second paragraph: " 'Here, caddie.' He hit. They went away across the pasture. I held to the fence and watched them going away." The novel appeared in 1929, the same year that saw the publication of *Sartoris*. With those two novels Faulkner introduced the world to the Sartoris and Compson families and the world of Yoknapatawpha County. He also introduced the reading public to the experimental writing techniques and inner and outer worlds of violence that characterized his fictional world of the Deep South. American literature has not been the same since. By 1931 his novels were being published in Great Britain, and his fame spread quickly, even though it was not until 1949 that he received the Nobel Prize for his work. He crowned his long career on that occasion with one of the finest acceptance speeches in the history of that international award.

*N*OW a traveler must make his way to Noon City by the best means he can, for there are no buses or trains heading in that direction, though six days a week a truck from the Chuberry Turpentine Company collects mail and supplies in the next-door town of Paradise Chapel: occasionally a person bound for Noon City can catch a ride with the driver of the truck, Sam Radclif. It's a rough trip no matter how you come, for these washboard roads will loosen up even brandnew cars pretty fast; and hitchhikers always find the going bad. Also, this is lonesome country; and here in the swamplike hollows where tiger lilies bloom the size of a man's head, there are luminous green logs that shine under the dark marsh water like drowned corpses; often the only movement on the landscape is winter smoke winding out the chimney of some sorry-looking farmhouse, or a wing-stiffened bird, silent and arrow-eyed, circling over the black deserted pinewoods.

ONE critic of Truman Capote's first novel, *Other Voices, Other Rooms*, described the event: "A twenty-three-year-old boy from New Orleans, with a wild lust for words and a poisonous imagination, tells what I hope will be the eeriest story of 1948." In comparison with Capote, he said, Faulkner "seems healthy and happy." Capote has become such a public figure and the object of so much attention that it is difficult to remember the impact on the reading public of this wondrously written novel of the Deep South, with its aura of mystery and potential horror, all caught in the opening paragraph. It would be unfortunate if reaction to the personality of the author were to hold any reader back from the experience of this moving story in which reality is slightly awry. If only for the love of verbal play and masterfully wrought sentences, the reader who has not encountered this book should seek to do so immediately—preferably on a dark night.

A DESTINY that leads the English to the Dutch is strange enough; but one that leads from Epsom into Pennsylvania, and thence into the hills that shut in Altamont over the proud coral cry of the cock, and the soft stone smile of an angel, is touched by that dark miracle of chance which makes new magic in a dusty world.

Each of us is all the sums he has not counted: subtract us into nakedness and night again, and you shall see begin in Crete four thousand years ago the love that ended yesterday in Texas.

The seed of our destruction will blossom in the desert, the alexin of our cure grows by a mountain rock, and our lives are haunted by a Georgia slattern, because a London cutpurse went unhung. Each moment is the fruit of forty thousand years. The minute-winning days, like flies, buzz home to death, and every moment is a window on all time.

BACK when I was in college, we used to play games like "What is the greatest work of art in history?" It may have been useless, even misguided, but it made us think. One of the great questions was "What is the great American novel?" The usual answer to that one was "None. It's still to be written." My answer was "the four novels of Thomas Wolfe." I'm still not sure I was wrong. The first paragraph of *Look Homeward, Angel* would have been sufficient to meet the guidelines of this collection, but as with most of Wolfe, you just can't stop with one sentence or one paragraph. Reading Wolfe is like eating salted peanuts. It is true that he suffers from verbal diarrhoea, but that only makes him more an American. He is a Faust eager for knowledge and experience, especially experience. It is true that you need to read him when you are a teenager to feel his full impact, but that youthfulness mirrors America's refusal to accept age as a virtue. His greatness is mirrored in this opening of his first novel, which appeared in 1929: he lives the present moment to the full, in good American style, but he always is aware of wider relationships. His present is lived in the full view of history. If his words flow too easily and repetitively, they also flow richly and fully. They are a cornucopia of thoughts and feelings. I fear that young people today will never share the sound that he and others like myself remember of the train whistle at night over great distances, full of loneliness and longing but also the call to adventure. I worry that they do not want to ravage visually dark libraries at night, alone with the treasures of the past. I fear that they do not want to wander the streets of Cambridge at night uttering goat cries—but think wolf whistles a suitable substitute. But I cease fearing when I see some college freshman or sophomore swept up in his tales, in his language, as I and my friends were. And I guess my real worry is that I find myself bogging down after the twentieth repetition of city dwellers being described as sidewalk ciphers. But then I come back to this wonderful opening of *Look Homeward, Angel,* or I think of the best thing he ever wrote, the title of his last book, *You Can't Go Home Again,* and I remain somewhat convinced of my earlier judgment of his work.

I'VE seen a corpse for the first time. It's Wednesday but I feel as if it were Sunday because I didn't go to school and they dressed me up in a green corduroy suit that's tight in some places. Holding Mama's hand, following my grandfather, who feels his way along with a cane with every step he takes so he won't bump into things (he doesn't see well in the dark and he limps), I went past the mirror in the living room and saw myself full length, dressed in green and with this white starched collar that pinches me on one side of the neck. I saw myself in the round mottled looking glass and I thought: *That's me, as if today was Sunday*.

CATCHING both the mood and intonation as well as the wording of childhood has been the goal of good writers in all ages, and not many have been successful. Gabriel Garcia Marquez has not only pulled it off in the opening sentence of *Leaf Storm* (in this 1972 English translation by Gregory Rabassa), but he has joined it with his usual near-fantasy view of reality that often borders on the macabre. Even the reader who has not read *Leaf Storm* should be able to identify the style and mood, as this story is from the tales of Macondo, the subject of Marquez's much more famous *One Hundred Years of Solitude*. The shock of the opening sentence is matched so well with the childlike detail of the following description that the reader has to keep going to find out who the corpse is that the child is going to see.

ON A hill by the Mississippi where Chippewas camped two generations ago, a girl stood in relief against the cornflower blue of Northern sky. She saw no Indians now; she saw flour-mills and the blinking windows of skyscrapers in Minneapolis and St. Paul. Nor was she thinking of squaws and portages, and the Yankee fur-traders whose shadows were all about her. She was meditating upon walnut fudge, the plays of Brieux, the reasons why heels run over, and the fact that the chemistry instructor had stared at the new coiffure which concealed her ears.

ALTHOUGH he had written five earlier novels, Sinclair Lewis's first real success was *Main Street,* published in 1920. In it he not only created a lasting view of small-town American society, but he gave it a name as well. He was describing a world he knew well, having grown up in the Middle West, and his portrayals of people and institutions have the crispness of line and acidic bite of an etching. Two years later he was to add to his view of America's cultural wasteland with *Babbitt.* With *Arrowsmith,* in 1925, Lewis won the Pulitzer Prize but refused to accept it; but when he was awarded the Nobel Prize for Literature in 1930, he willingly made the trip to Stockholm. His penetrating views of American life had won him a well-deserved international reputation. It is a bit surprising that there has not been a resurgence of public interest in *Main Street,* for the heroine, Carol Milford, is a fine study of the way social pressures turn a girl with a good mind into just another married woman in the small-town society of Gopher Prairie. Lewis sums up her problem nicely: "she was a woman with a working brain and no work." And in the end the small-town society and its small thoughts drag her down to their level. Lewis, as with the character of Babbitt, is not attacking Carol. His judgment lies against the society that debilitates a basically good person. Whether the situation has changed as much as many critics would have us believe is a matter for thought for any reader. If Gopher Prairie was only fifty years away from pioneer settlement, much of the country is still less than one hundred years away from pioneer days and still contains many of the same signs and attitudes that Lewis described. A leather and handcraft shop on the main street does not a civilization make.

*I*N 1926 I was enrolled as student airline pilot by the Latécoère Company, the predecessors of Aeropostale (now Air France) in the operation of the line between Toulouse, in southwestern France, and Dakar, in French West Africa. I was learning the craft, undergoing an apprenticeship served by all young pilots before they were allowed to carry the mails. We took ships up on trial spins, made meek little hops between Toulouse and Perpignan, and had dreary lessons in meteorology in a freezing hangar. We lived in fear of the mountains of Spain, over which we had yet to fly, and in awe of our elders.

THERE is not a great deal in this opening paragraph to herald the adventure of thought and language that lies ahead after that beginning—except perhaps for the wonderfully quiet choice of "meek" and "dreary" as descriptive adjectives, and the adept use of "elders" to indicate the attitude of a neophyte in any incipient endeavor. The author, Antoine de Saint Exupéry, has caught the glory, the mystery, and the tangible fear of flying better than any other writer, in a trilogy of which *Wind, Sand and Stars*, published in America in 1939, is the first volume. Anyone who first came to know Exupéry through his work *The Little Prince* will be just as delighted in his books on the adventure of flying. The reader will find the same depth of perception of the human condition: "The machine which at first blush seems a means of isolating man from the great problems of nature, actually plunges him more deeply into them." And there is the same sense of poetry: "A cliff on the edge of the airdrome stood in profile against the sky as if it were daylight." Halfway through the novel, Exupéry wrote what could easily be his own epitaph: ". . . when a man dies, an unknown world passes away." When, during World War II, Exupéry took off from an Italian airport and headed north into oblivion, he made us all realize how little we had known him. Yet we can rejoice that he revealed as much as he did in his books.

A RATHER handsome, light traveling carriage on springs rolled into the gates of an inn in a certain provincial capital, the kind of carriage that is favored by bachelors: retired lieutenant-colonels, second captains, landowners possessing a hundred souls or so of serfs—in a word, all those who are called the fair-to-middlin' sort. The gentleman seated in this carriage was no Adonis, but he wasn't bad to look at, either; he was neither too stout nor too thin; you couldn't say he was old, but still he wasn't what you might call any too young, either. His arrival created no stir whatever in the town of N—— and was not coupled with any remarkable event; all the comments it called forth came from two native muzhiks standing in the doorway of a pot-house across the way from the inn, comments which, however, had more to do with the carriage itself than with the man sitting in it.

THE opening of Nikolai Gogol's *Dead Souls*, published in 1842, is a remarkable setting of character, title, and theme. The remarkable element is not that a writer would try to get so much into an opening paragraph but that he accomplishes it with so little fanfare: everything about the description seems so ordinary. But the hero, Chichikov, is the man in the carriage; his wealth being described in terms of the possession of "souls" or serfs, alive or dead, is the source of both the title and the plot of this novel of the corruption of landowners and the devaluation of human life in Russia. The use of a carriage to set a social message prepares for the shift by the end of the book to the use of the troika, the three-horse carriage of Russia, that Chichikov rides in at the end, rejoicing in the speed. No Russian could have helped but be moved by the peroration that Gogol delivers in such sentences as "And art not thou, my Russia, soaring along even like a spirited, never-to-be-outdistanced troika?" and "With a wondrous ring does the jingle-bell trill; the air, rent to shreds, thunders and turns to wind; all things on earth fly past and, eying it askance, all the peoples and nations stand aside and give it the right of way." That prophecy turned sour later in the century, when Dostoyevsky would describe the ending as being "either in an excess of childish and naive optimism, or simply in fear of the censorship of the day." But when one is reading the novel, he is caught up in Gogol's enthusiasm; and Gogol was no more chauvinistic than most authors of the century.

*A*S Gregor Samsa awoke one morning from uneasy dreams he found himself transformed in his bed into a gigantic insect. He was lying on his hard, as it were armor-plated, back and when he lifted his head a little he could see his dome-like brown belly divided into stiff arched segments on top of which the bed quilt could hardly keep in position and was about to slide off completely. His numerous legs, which were pitifully thin compared to the rest of his bulk, waved helplessly before his eyes.

ALTHOUGH all of us suffer from various degrees of guilt at different times in our life, few of us are forced into seeing ourselves turned into a gigantic cockroach as a result. It takes the imagination of Franz Kafka to do that. Written in 1912 (published in 1915), this story runs remarkably parallel to the outspoken letter he wrote to his father in 1919 about his feelings of guilt and paralysis in relationship to that stern gentleman. Probably nowhere else in literature is there a better fictional portrayal of the Oedipus complex. Only as perceptive a person and as perfect a stylist as Kafka could make such a transformation believable to the reader. (It takes its title *Metamorphosis* from Ovid's famous recounting of the mythical changes in classical mythology.) And believable and frightening and pathetic it is. The story is too long to be considered a short story and not long enough to fall into the category of a novel. It occupies that literary region of obscure classification known as the novella, and it shares the classification with such great works as Dostoyevsky's *Notes from Underground,* Mann's *Death in Venice,* and Conrad's *Heart of Darkness.* Readers are fortunate that writers discovered that middle ground, for all of these works place an emotional load on the reader that would be intolerable at any greater length.

*I*T WAS a bright cold day in April, and the clocks were striking thirteen. Winston Smith, his chin muzzled into his breast in an effort to escape the vile wind, slipped quickly through the glass doors of Victory Mansions, though not quickly enough to prevent a swirl of gritty dust from entering along with him.

GEORGE Orwell sets the stage for his pessimistic view of *1984* with considerable subtlety. The only point that sets his 1949 novel opening slightly askew is the chiming of the clocks. The title of the apartment house could easily come from any postwar era, and the gritty dust is with us always—although it is a quick way of saying that the world is less than we could wish it to be. The next paragraph takes us more obviously into the future with the omnipresent poster BIG BROTHER IS WATCHING YOU! For many readers Orwell's novel is the most frightening of the prophetic books of our century. For anyone who has read the book, the year 1984 has stood as a worrisome signpost, even as we have lived through it. Orwell had learned from Huxley's *Brave New World* that the future is nearer than we think. Perhaps, as we experienced 1984, we may feel he picked a date too close to the time of his novel, but perhaps not. Certainly the principles of Newspeak, in which public words take on their opposite meaning (War is Peace, Freedom is Slavery, Ignorance is Strength), are already fully at work in our society. The Vietnam war witnessed that bastardization of the language at its height, and daily statements from all of the capitals of the world continue to show the validity of Orwell's prophecy about language. The mental coercion that is the most frightening aspect of the book has been proven accurate in the undercover activities of every major power in the world. If it has not yet risen to the surface of daily life, we may perhaps be able to thank Orwell for holding back the process by publicizing its effects as well as he did in his novel.

*O*NE Christmas was so much like another, in those years around the sea-town corner now and out of all sound except the distant speaking of the voices I sometimes hear a moment before sleep, that I can never remember whether it snowed for six days and six nights when I was twelve or whether it snowed for twelve days and twelve nights when I was six.

ONCE again, I suppose I have cheated the reader. I suppose I should have used the sentence-paragraph: "I like very much people telling me about their childhood, but they'll have to be quick or else I'll be telling them about mine." But the first sentence of "A Child's Christmas in Wales" is so delightful, so typically Dylan Thomas, that I couldn't help myself. Besides, each of the segments of *Quite Early One Morning*, published in 1954, is actually a work in itself. The first section, "Reminiscences of Childhood," merely sets the stage for each of the individual pieces that follow. Thomas's lyric voice revealed itself in everything he wrote, whether in prose or poetry. For anyone who has heard Thomas read in public or listened to any of his recordings, it becomes nigh unto impossible to read him without trying to mimic the rolling sonority of his voice and its cadences. It is akin to listening to a Welsh choir warming up to one of their magnificent hymns. In the case of "A Child's Christmas in Wales," the beginning sets perfectly the light and marvelously humorous tone of the whole piece, in which cats, "sleek and long as jaguars and horrible-whiskered," "slink and sidle over the white back-garden walls." Or Jim's aunt, Miss Prothero, standing in the midst of a chaos of firemen, hose-water, and melting snowballs, inquires brightly, "Would you like anything to read?" We read and we find images of our own childhood rushing back to fill the void between sentences—and we wish we had the words and the imagination to bring our memories to life as Thomas brought his own childhood to life so that we could share in it.

74

*T*HE cold passed reluctantly from the earth, and the retiring fogs revealed an army stretched out on the hills, resting. As the landscape changed from brown to green, the army awakened, and began to tremble with eagerness at the noise of rumors. It cast its eyes upon the roads, which were growing from long troughs of liquid mud to proper thoroughfares. A river, amber-tinted in the shadow of its banks, purled at the army's feet; and at night, when the stream had become of a sorrowful blackness, one could see across it the red, eyelike gleam of hostile camp-fires set in the low brows of distant hills.

As THE sun begins to rise over the Civil War battlefield, the reader is about to meet a group of men to whom he is introduced only by external characteristics: the tall soldier, a corporal, the blatant soldier, a fat soldier, and, most important, a young soldier, the hero of the novel *The Red Badge of Courage*. Torn from the individual lives of civilian life (it is in a dream sequence of home that "Henry" is individualized by his name), these men take on the characteristics of all men in battle. And our hero must face the same fears, the same desire to escape from certain death, that all soldiers in war must face. The fact that he gives in to his fears and deserts his company during the onslaught of the enemy never causes us to lose sympathy with him. But because we can understand his fears and his unwillingness to die as just another piece of cannon fodder, we can also rejoice with him as he wins his badge of courage by returning to his company and acting with genuine bravery by the end of the book. Stephen Crane was born six years after the end of the Civil War and had never seen a battle. But when he published his war novel in 1895, he gave to the world a model by which to judge real cowardice or real bravery. And most war novels since that time, at least most American war novels, have been based to some degree on Crane's insights and techniques. Hemingway, for example, holds off from giving the names of his soldiers in *A Farewell to Arms* in much the same way that Crane did in this book. It is a powerful way to depict the faceless mass of men who go to their deaths in major wars.

*T*HE cell door slammed behind Rubashov.

BETWEEN 1938 and 1940 Arthur Koestler wrote his story of the Moscow purges of the 1930s, *Darkness at Noon*. As he said about his book, the characters are fictional but the events are real. This was the book that introduced the West to the horrors of political trials and imprisonment in Russia. There were many who felt that it was an extreme statement, and Koestler came under attack from those who were arguing for cooperation between the major powers during World War II and afterwards. Liberals tended to feel that Koestler was either overstating the problem or that he was describing a situation that had become less extreme. Then the events in Hungary in 1956 and in Czechoslovakia in 1968 took place and made Koestler's description very contemporary. Finally, with the publication of *The Gulag Archipelago*, the world was shown how accurate the novel that Koestler had written in the late 1930s actually was—and remains. The story of the survival of the manuscript of the book is almost as exciting as the novel. Koestler wrote the book in Paris, in German. After he had finished the work, the police raided his apartment and took away all of his manuscripts, but missed the manuscript of *Darkness at Noon*. Later, he was again arrested, and the German manuscript was confiscated. By then, however, an English translation had been completed, and that was sent off to London for publication just ten days before the Nazis entered Paris. Koestler spent six months finding a way to escape to England, and he was in jail in that country, under suspicion, when the book appeared in print in 1941.

*O*N Friday noon, July the twentieth, 1714, the finest bridge in all Peru broke and precipitated five travellers into the gulf below. This bridge was on the high-road between Lima and Cuzco and hundreds of persons passed over it every day. It had been woven of osier by the Incas more than a century before and visitors to the city were always led out to see it. It was a mere ladder of thin slats swung out over the gorge, with handrails of dried vine. Horses and coaches and chairs had to go down hundreds of feet below and pass over the narrow torrent on rafts, but not one, not even the Viceroy, not even the Archbishop of Lima, had descended with the baggage rather than cross by the famous bridge. . . . St. Louis of France himself protected it, by his name and by the little mud church on the further side. The bridge seemed to be among the things that last forever; it was unthinkable that it should break. The moment a Peruvian heard of the accident he signed himself and made a mental calculation as to how recently he had crossed by it and how soon he had intended crossing by it again. People wandered about in a trance-like state, muttering; they had the hallucination of seeing themselves falling into a gulf.

THE marked hiatus in the middle of the paragraph is, of course, an attempt to add a slight bit of mystery to the identity of the book which begins with this opening description, which blends the style of a newspaper report and a human response to such an act of fate, chance, or destiny. The name of the bridge is that of the book itself, *The Bridge of San Luis Rey*, written in 1927 by Thornton Wilder. The remainder of the book deals with the patient search by Brother Juniper into the lives and characters of the five persons who perished in the accident in order to try to discover what it was that led God to choose them to perish together in this common accident. Wilder has hit on a subject that anyone with any religious leanings whatever has pondered at one time or another: Why does God choose certain persons for what seem mindless or purposeless acts of chance? If Wilder's conclusion does not satisfy every reader, it is certainly a result of the fact that there is no answer—at least no answer that any human can discover.

"YES, of course, if it's fine tomorrow," said Mrs. Ramsay. "But you'll have to be up with the lark," she added.

To her son these words conveyed an extraordinary joy, as if it were settled, the expedition were bound to take place, and the wonder to which he had looked forward, for years and years it seemed, was, after a night's darkness and a day's sail, within touch. Since he belonged, even at the age of six, to that great clan which cannot keep this feeling separate from that, but must let future prospects, with their joys and sorrows, cloud what is actually at hand, since to such people even in earliest childhood any turn in the wheel of sensation has the power to crystallise and transfix the moment upon which its gloom or radiance rests, James Ramsay, sitting on the floor cutting out pictures from the illustrated catalogue of the Army and Navy Stores, endowed the picture of a refrigerator, as his mother spoke, with heavenly bliss. It was fringed with joy. The wheelbarrow, the lawnmower, the sound of poplar trees, leaves whitening before rain, rooks cawing, brooms knocking, dresses rustling—all these were so coloured and distinguished in his mind that he had already his private code, his secret language, though he appeared the image of stark and uncompromising severity, with his high forehead and his fierce blue eyes, impeccably candid and pure, frowning slightly at the sight of human frailty, so that his mother, watching him guide his scissors neatly around the refrigerator, imagined him all red and ermine on the Bench or directing a stern and momentous enterprise in some crisis of public affairs.

THE journey that young James Ramsay is looking forward to is *To the Lighthouse*, the 1927 novel of interior and exterior landscapes by Virginia Woolf. Woolf, the daughter of Leslie Stephen, the great nineteenth-century author, scholar, and inaugurator of the monumental *Dictionary of National Biography*, had already completed four novels when she undertook *To the Lighthouse*. In each her approach was different, but as she developed, she became, with James Joyce, one of the real innovators of "stream of consciousness" writing. The opening paragraph not only sets the plot: the preparation for and the actual trip out to the lighthouse which stands visible on the horizon straight out from the Ramsay house; it also lets the reader know that it is not by action that the novel will progress, but by the thoughts that pass through the minds of the characters in the novel, especially the mind of Mrs. Ramsay. Actual conversation is secondary to interior dialogue or monologue. And even the arrival at the lighthouse, shrouded in mist, is achieved not in a visible boat but in the mind of Mrs. Ramsay. Unfortunately, it must be admitted that most people know Virginia Woolf not from her books, but from the title of Edward Albee's famous play and movie, *Who's Afraid of Virginia Woolf?* Unless the viewer or reader of that play knows that Woolf is the arch-portrayer of the emotions of the inner life that only rarely rise to the surface, he will never understand the brilliance of the title. And unless he understands that, he may never turn to the woman who turned our inner lives into mystical and mysterious wonders, from children who can endow photographs of refrigerators with heavenly bliss to women who, in their contemplation of the lives around them, can say, "I have had my vision."

*O*NCE upon a time, in a gloomy castle on a lonely hill, where there were thirteen clocks that wouldn't go, there lived a cold, aggressive Duke, and his niece, the Princess Saralinda. She was warm in every wind and weather, but he was always cold. His hands were as cold as his smile and almost as cold as his heart. He wore gloves when he was asleep, and he wore gloves when he was awake, which made it difficult for him to pick up pins or coins or the kernels of nuts, or to tear the wings from nightingales. He was six feet four, and forty-six, and even colder than he thought he was. One eye wore a velvet patch; the other glittered through a monocle, which made half his body seem closer to you than the other half. He had lost one eye when he was twelve, for he was fond of peering into nests and lairs in search of birds and animals to maul. One afternoon, a mother shrike had mauled him first. His nights were spent in evil dreams, and his days were given to wicked schemes.

IF I may be allowed to paraphrase, many children's books, like childhood, are wasted on children. That does not mean, of course, that children don't like the works, but that adults can gain even more pleasure from them. It is not surprising, therefore, that so many fine writers take it upon themselves to write children's books. Two of the finest prose stylists in American literature, James Thurber and E. B. White, are examples of that predilection. The present example is the opening paragraph of Thurber's marvelous *The 13 Clocks*, written in 1950. The book, written in prose form, is sheer poetry. It is tempting to quote huge gobs of the work to prove that the sheer delight in sound that is already apparent in the beginning paragraph permeates the entire book, but it would mean quoting the whole thing. So I will limit myself to one other paragraph:

> The brambles and the thorns grew thick and thicker in a ticking thicket of bickering crickets. Farther along and stronger, bonged the gongs of a throng of frogs, green and vivid on their lily pads. From the sky came the crying of flies, and the pilgrims leaped over a bleating sheep creeping knee-deep in a sleepy stream, in which swift and slippery snakes slid and slithered silkily, whispering sinful secrets.

If that doesn't send the reader who has never seen the book scurrying off to the library and bookstore, nothing else I might say ever will.

*A*T THE Court of an Emperor (he lived it matters not when) there was among the many gentlewomen of the Wardrobe and Chamber one, who though she was not of very high rank was favoured far beyond all the rest; so that the great ladies of the Palace, each of whom had secretly hoped that she herself would be chosen, looked with scorn and hatred upon the upstart who had dispelled their dreams. Still less were her former companions, the minor ladies of the Wardrobe, content to see her raised so far above them. Thus her position at Court, preponderant though it was, exposed her to constant jealousy and ill will; and soon, worn out with petty vexations, she fell into a decline, growing very melancholy and retiring frequently to her home. But the Emperor, so far from wearying of her now that she was no longer well or gay, grew every day more tender, and paid not the smallest heed to those who reproved him, till his conduct became the talk of all the land; and even his own barons and courtiers began to look askance at an attachment so ill-advised. They whispered among themselves that in the Land Beyond the Sea such happenings had led to riot and disaster. The people of the country did indeed soon have many grievances to show: and some likened her to Yang Kuei-fei, the mistress of Ming Huang. Yet, for all this discontent, so great was the sheltering power of master's love that none dared openly molest her.

AMERICANS and Westerners in general tend to be extremely myopic when it comes to cultural history. This volume has been filled with statements like "the first novel is . . ." But the novel had been around for centuries in the Orient. For many readers the best example of that earlier group is *The Tale of Genji*, by Lady Murasaki, who was born about 978 A.D. Her novel was written over a number of years, but it was apparently finished by 1022 A.D., probably sometime during the last decade of her life. She disappears from the court records by 1031. Her tale of life at the Japanese court was based on long familiarity, and although it begins with the blend of history and fairy tale that was usual in the works that preceded her, it becomes a genuine novel, filled with the intrigue, amours, and military activities of the age. For anyone who wants to gain a genuine knowledge of early Japan, there is no more pleasant or entertaining way of gaining that knowledge than reading *The Tale of Genji*.

A THRONG of bearded men, in sad-colored garments and gray, steeple-crowned hats, intermixed with women, some wearing hoods, and others bareheaded, was assembled in front of a wooden edifice, the door of which was heavily timbered with oak, and studded with iron spikes.

The founders of a new colony, whatever Utopia of human virtue and happiness they might originally project, have invariably recognized it among their earliest practical necessities to allot a portion of the virgin soil as a cemetery, and another portion as the site of a prison. . . .

FOR the readers who know the book, the first paragraph is enough; they already know that the wooden edifice is a prison. But the beginning of the second paragraph not only provides that information for the unknowing but also the irony that touches everything that Nathaniel Hawthorne had to say about his puritan forebears. The colony of pilgrim fathers who had wanted to found a New Jerusalem on virgin soil brought with them plenty of conviction of original and actual sin, and that required a jail for the likes of Hester Prynne, the long-suffering heroine of *The Scarlet Letter*, Hawthorne's most famous novel. It was begun in 1849 and published the next year, at the beginning of the outpouring of great works of American literature which took place in the 1850s. It is a model of the historical novel. Not only is the story of Hester and her child—and that child's loving but weak father—gripping in itself, but the novel gives us one of our best pictures of life in the Puritan colonies. It was a life that was morally cramped in spite of the openness of the new American landscape. Hawthorne could never excuse his own ancestors for the role they played in the witch trials of the colonies, nor could he forgive them for the rigidity of their religious code which froze the lifeblood of young and lively colonists. In the midst of that moral climate, Hester stands strong and unbending, a model for all who would stand by their own inner values in the face of society's tyranny.

I WAS walking by the Thames. Half-past morning on an autumn day. Sun in a mist. Like an orange in a fried fish shop. All bright below. Low tide, dusty water and a crooked bar of straw, chicken boxes, dirt and oil from mud to mud. Like a viper swimming in skim milk. The old serpent, symbol of nature and love.

To a keen reader this opening reveals not a poet's eye, but an artist's eye. Color and visual effects are the dominant notes. And well that might be in this 1944 novel by Joyce Cary, *The Horse's Mouth*, for the main character is the lusty, exuberant sixty-seven-year-old artist Gully Jimson. As one reviewer at the time said, it is difficult to decide whether the book is a satire, a comedy, or a farcical tragedy. It is also difficult to understand why it took five years for American publishers to recognize its power after it had appeared in England. Perhaps it is due to the fact that Jimson is so irreverent, so untrammeled by the mores of society, so free of any feelings of guilt, so unmoved by traditional attitudes about personal possession and private property that the publishers were afraid of the public response (a situation remarkably paralleled in later years by the treatment of the manuscript of *A Confederacy of Dunces*). But there is far more to this book than the story. There is visual imagery run riot: "The moon was coming up somewhere, round the corner from the side bow window, making the trees like fossils in a coalfield . . . It was like a working model of the earth before somebody thought of dirt, and colors and birds and humans." For anyone interested in having his senses challenged, *The Horse's Mouth* remains an exciting experience. The famous movie, even with the presence of Alec Guinness, is no substitute.

*I*T WAS the best of times, it was the worst of times, it was the age of wisdom, it was the age of foolishness, it was the epoch of belief, it was the epoch of incredulity, it was the season of Light, it was the season of Darkness, it was the spring of hope, it was the winter of despair, we had everything before us, we had nothing before us, we were all going direct to Heaven, we were all going direct the other way—in short, the period was so far like the present period, that some of its noisiest authorities insisted on its being received, for good or for evil, in the superlative degree of comparison only.

I DESCRIBED the opening sentence of *Anna Karenina* earlier as perhaps the most famous beginning of a novel in history. For many readers, especially those whose major reading of novels took place during their school years, that may not be true; instead, this beginning sentence-paragraph of Charles Dickens's *A Tale of Two Cities* holds that august position. The classical balances of the sentence are certainly striking, and the simple wording of the first two clauses are what remain in most readers' minds from their high-school English classes. Dickens first thought about a novel on the subject of the French Revolution in 1857 and started to work using Carlyle's history of *The French Revolution* as well as other works as a basis. As he was later to say, "I read no books but such as had the air of the time in them" while he was at work on the book, which appeared in 1859, nine years and four novels after his favorite work, *David Copperfield*. His goal of portraying the age of the Revolution was remarkably successful, just as his holding off the identity of his hero until well into the second book of the volume was successful in drawing his reader into the novel with action-filled suspense. The opening nicely states the English view of the Revolutionary period from a midcentury position, but it also makes a remarkably apt statement about the way all of us view the age in which we ourselves live: the best of times and the worst of times.

*T*O *THE* red country and part of the gray country of Oklahoma, the last rains came gently, and they did not cut the scarred earth. The plows crossed and recrossed the rivulet marks. The last rains lifted the corn quickly and scattered weed colonies and grass along the sides of the roads so that the gray country and the dark red country began to disappear under a green cover. In the last part of May the sky grew pale and the clouds that had hung in high puffs for so long in the spring were dissipated. The sun flared down on the growing corn day after day until a line of brown spread along the edge of each green bayonet. The clouds appeared, and went away, and in a while they did not try any more. The weeds grew darker green to protect themselves, and they did not spread any more. The surface of the earth crusted, a thin hard crust, and as the sky became pale, so the earth became pale, pink in the red country and white in the gray country.

ANY attempt to describe life in the United States during the Great Depression years of the 1930s has to include one or more passages from John Steinbeck's wonderful novel of the Joad family and their fellow refugees from the dust bowl of Oklahoma and north Texas, *The Grapes of Wrath,* published in 1939 while the effects of that mass migration from the devastating effects of the drought were still being felt. Images from the book have become part of our national heritage, from the turtle struggling manfully across the highway in chapter three, to the helpless tenant farmer with his rifle trying to halt the progress of the tractor across his land in chapter five, to the empty farm houses, whose "doors . . . swung open, and drifted back and forth in the wind" in chapter eleven. All Hollywood had to do to make one of its greatest films was to transfer to celluloid the images of the book. Unfortunately, the film makers did not have the courage to reproduce clearly the final scene as Rose of Sharon suckles the starved older man who has given up hope. But in that act of love and succor, the young girl restores hope not only to the man, but to the country that was struggling to return to some sort of normalcy and human caring.

O_{NE} thing was certain, that the *white* kitten had had nothing to do with it—it was the black kitten's fault entirely. For the white kitten had been having its face washed by the old cat for the last quarter of an hour (and bearing it pretty well, considering): so you see that it *couldn't* have had any hand in the mischief.

As ALMOST everyone knows, the resident fellow in Mathematics at Christ Church, Oxford, Charles Dodgson, spent July 4, 1862, entertaining three little girls named Liddell in a rowboat on the Isis River by telling them stories. One of the girls, a ten-year-old named Alice, became the heroine of those stories and therefore the heroine of the most popular of all children's books. I have picked the opening of the second of the stories, *Through the Looking-Glass*, partly because it is not as familiar as the opening of *Alice in Wonderland* and partly because the latter work begins by giving away the heroine's name. I also picked it because Dodgson, or Lewis Carroll, as he signed his name to the books, put so many excellent remarks about the English language into that second work, appearing the first time in 1872, seven years after the first. Not only is the best nonsense poem in the English language, "Jabberwocky," in the *Looking-Glass*, but so are the delightful discussion about the nature of reality in the conversation with Tweedledum and Tweedledee and the best discussion of language I know of in any book in the argument with Humpty Dumpty:

> "When *I* use a word," Humpty Dumpty said, in rather a scornful tone, "it means just what I choose it to mean—neither more nor less."
> "The question is," said Alice, "whether you *can* make words mean so many different things."
> "The question is," said Humpty Dumpty, "which is to be master—that's all."

Anyone who is misled into thinking that the playful kittens of the opening are an introduction to a mere child's tale will miss one of the most remarkable reading experiences offered in English literature. I find it amusing, at the very least, that most libraries place this book in the children's literature section rather than in the section devoted to English fiction.

*W**E WERE* in class when the head-master came in, followed by a "new fellow," not wearing the school uniform, and a
school servant carrying a large desk. Those who had been asleep
woke up, and every one rose as if just surprised at his work.

IT IS not surprising, as we learn during the course of the novel, that the opening paragraph of *Madame Bovary*, published by Gustave Flaubert in 1856, does not deal with the leading character in the novel. As a matter of fact, Emma Bovary does not appear until some thirteen pages later, well into chapter two. Flaubert, perhaps the greatest stylist in the French language, was not making an error in judgment. Emma's life and death can only be understood in the framework of rural life in northern France and in the context of marriage to the unimaginative, dull boy who arrives in the classroom in the first paragraph of the book. Emma, sensuous, sentimental, and sensitive, has no defenses against the dullness, tawdriness, and monotony of small-town life. Flaubert and his publisher were in court by January of 1857, defending themselves against the charge of "outrage of public morals and religion." They were quickly acquitted, and the case actually helped sell the new book—a not infrequent result of such cases. The charges were obviously ridiculous, for the novel would hardly suggest to any reader that it would be a good idea to follow Emma as a model. It is certainly true that we sympathize with her situation and dilemma. We may even find ourselves agreeing with Flaubert's statement: "Madame Bovary, c'est moi." But we do not need to know Aristotle to realize that a bad choice of means almost invariably leads to a bad end. Perhaps even more importantly, the novel makes us realize that although it is a story of a mid-nineteenth-century French heroine, her situation is as modern as the latest rural newspaper story or the latest report of a city divorce case.

"WELL, Prince, so Genoa and Lucca are now just family estates of the Buonapartes. But I warn you, if you don't tell me that this means war, if you still try to defend the infamies and horrors perpetrated by that Antichrist—I really believe he is Antichrist—I will have nothing more to do with you and you are no longer my friend, no longer my 'faithful slave,' as you call yourself! But how do you do? I see I have frightened you—sit down and tell me all the news."

IT IS tempting to devote an entire page to remarks about this work made by other writers. John Galsworthy, E. M. Forster, Hugh Walpole, Turgenev, Mark Van Doren, Van Wyck Brooks, and dozens of others have called it the greatest novel ever written. It would have to appear in any list of the ten most important works of fiction in any language. It also would be in any list of the longest novels in history, which is one reason that more people have not read it. Leo Tolstoy began *War and Peace* in 1863, a year after he was married, and the first part was published in 1865. It was not until 1869 that the final part appeared in print. Thus it took almost as long a time to write the book than the actual narrated events covered: Anna Scherer's opening remarks to Prince Vasili Kuragin took place in July 1805, and the book ends with the return of the Russians to Moscow in late 1812 and early 1813. The panorama of life that unfolds in the 1300-plus pages of the novel is as colorful as it is overwhelming. The title of the novel does not claim too much; it is indeed a full picture of war and peace. But Tolstoy's purpose is a great deal wider in scope than the simple narrative, no matter how all-inclusive that might be. For over half a century Europe had been living under the shadow of the superman Napoleon. Unlike Anna Scherer, most nineteenth-century readers shared a view of Napoleon as a man who was above the laws and standards of morality of ordinary men. Dostoyevsky, in 1866, was writing a novel to investigate the claims of such extraordinary men. Carlyle had turned the concept into a justification for Captains of Industry who were not restrained by ordinary humanitarian considerations. And Tolstoy wanted to challenge the Great Man theory of history. His novel was to show that Napoleon was no more a man who determined history than his little-known Russian opponent Kutuzov; both were the products of history itself, not the other way around. Tolstoy constructed his novel around inner chapters of historical argument, in much the same way as Melville had built *Moby Dick* around inner chapters of whaling history and technique. Unfortunately, most readers are alienated by the historical analysis. That is too bad, as Tolstoy felt the importance of his work rested on that argument. Those who simply want the story can skip those chapters; but it is a mistake to do so.

*A*LEXEY Fyodorovich Karamazov was the third son of Fyodor Pavlovich Karamazov, a landowner well known in our district in his own day (and still remembered among us) owing to his tragic and obscure death, which happened exactly thirteen years ago, and which I shall describe in its proper place. For the present I will only say that this "landowner"—for so we used to call him, although he hardly lived on his own estate at all—was a strange type, yet one pretty frequently to be met with, a trashy and depraved type, and, in addition, senseless. But he was one of those senseless persons who are very well capable of looking after their worldy affairs, and, apparently, after nothing else. Fyodor Pavlovich, for instance, began with next to nothing; his estate was of the smallest; he ran to dine at other men's tables, and fastened on them as a toady, yet at his death it appeared that he had a hundred thousand rubles in hard cash. At the same time, he was all his life one of the most senseless madcaps in the whole district. I repeat, it was not stupidity—the majority of these foolish fellows are shrewd and intelligent enough—but just senselessness, and a peculiar and national form of it.

I suppose that I should have obscured the identity of the novel by eliminating the last name of the man whose three sons, Dmitri, Ivan, and Alyosha, make up the title of the novel *The Brothers Karamazov*. But that would have been too "cute" an approach for a book of this stature. Every collector of great passages has, it seems to me, the privilege of choosing his own favorite, and the place of honor for such a choice is legitimately the last in the book. I have already named some of the writers who have described *War and Peace* as the greatest novel ever written, but a very large number of readers reserve that praise for Dostoyevsky's final novel, *The Brothers Karamazov*, completed just two months before his death in January 1881. It is a superb mystery story, a major work of characterization, and one of the best theological treatises in the whole field of fiction. In the figure of Ivan, Dostoyevsky created perhaps his best example of the type of character he described as "The Double." The Grand Inquisitor scene is one of the greatest religious "stories" to be found outside of the Bible. The youngest of the brothers, Alyosha, or more formally Alexey, was to be the hero of the next novel that Dostoyevsky planned: *The Great Sinner*. As he comes close to being a saint in *The Brothers Karamazov*, most readers are amazed at the author's plans. But many readers find him the hero of this book as well. It is certainly true that Ivan wins all of the arguments in which these two brothers become involved, but, as one critic rightly observed, "Alyosha wins the book." At the end of the novel, Alyosha joins hands with the young boys that circle him, " 'And always so, all our lives hand in hand! Hurrah for Karamazov!' Kolya cried once more rapturously and once more all the boys chimed in." And the reader who has been caught up in the wonder of Dostoyevsky's great work joins in as well, "Hurrah for Karamazov!"

ACKNOWLEDGMENTS

We gratefully acknowledge the following permissions:

SAUL BELLOW. From *Henderson the Rain King*. Copyright © 1958, 1959, 1974, by Saul Bellow. Reprinted by permission of Viking Penguin Inc. and Harriet Wasserman Literary Agency, Inc.

ALBERT CAMUS. From *The Stranger*, translated by Stuart Gilbert. Reprinted by permission of Alfred A. Knopf, Inc.

TRUMAN CAPOTE. From *Other Voices, Other Rooms*. Copyright 1948 by Truman Capote. Reprinted by permission of Random House, Inc. and William Heinemann Ltd.

JOYCE CARY. From *The Horse's Mouth*. Copyright 1944 by Joyce Cary. Reprinted by permission of Harper & Row, Publishers, Inc.

FYODOR DOSTOYEVSKY. From *The Brothers Karamozov*, translated by Constance Garnett, published by Random House, Inc.

WILLIAM FAULKNER. From *The Sound and the Fury*. Copyright 1929 and renewed 1957 by William Faulkner. Reprinted by permission of Random House, Inc. and of Curtis Brown, London.

F. SCOTT FITZGERALD. From *The Great Gatsby*. Copyright 1925 Charles Scribner's Sons; copyright renewed. Reprinted with the permission of Charles Scribner's Sons and The Bodley Head.

NICOLAI V. GOGOL. From *Dead Souls*, edited by René Wellek, translated by B.G. Guerney, published by Holt, Rinehart and Winston.

ERNEST HEMINGWAY. From *A Farewell to Arms*. Copyright 1929 Charles Scribner's Sons; copyright renewed 1957 Ernest Hemingway. Reprinted with the permission of Charles Scribner's Sons, the Executors of the Ernest Hemingway Estate, and Jonathan Cape Ltd.

ALDOUS HUXLEY. From *Brave New World*. Copyright © 1932, 1960 by Aldous Huxley. Reprinted by permission of Harper & Row, Publishers, Inc.

FRANZ KAFKA. From *The Castle, Definitive Edition*, translated by Edwin and Willa Muir and Eithne Wilkins and Ernst Kaiser. Reprinted by permission of Alfred A. Knopf, Inc. and Martin Secker & Warburg Ltd.